THE CHRISTMAS STORY
FOR CHILDREN

Written by Yvonne Holloway McCall
Illustrated by Betty Wind

ARCH Books
Copyright © 1976 CONCORDIA PUBLISHING HOUSE, ST. LOUIS, MISSOURI
MANUFACTURED IN THE UNITED STATES OF AMERICA
ALL RIGHTS RESERVED
ISBN 0-570-06112-1

The innkeeper rushed.
He was in such a hurry.
All he had time for was money and worry.
In his little hotel
The nooks and the crannies
Were jammed full of children,
And parents and grannies.
He growled as he answered
A knock on the door.
He didn't have room for anyone more.

He peered at a man in the shadowy light
And a woman and donkey alone in the night.

"My wife," said the man, "is weary and worn,
For you see, her baby's about to be born."
"No room," the busy innkeeper said.
And he showed it was so
By a shake of his head.

"I'm sorry. I'd like to help and be kind,
But I simply have too much else on my mind.
Although," he mused,
"In the barn you could stay.
It's there in the back, out of the way.
It isn't exactly a first-class hotel.
There are flies and dirt,
And the animals smell,

But take it or leave it.
It's all that I've got."
And the man in the shadows
Sighed at the thought.
But he went and made pillows
Of hay in the stable
For Mary, his wife, as best he was able.

And the innkeeper went
To his own cozy suite
And then made sure he had plenty to eat.

Then he went back to working
As fast as he could
And did all the things
That an innkeeper should.

And shepherds were working
A night shift, as well,
When an angel appeared
With a story to tell.
He stood in their midst
In a shimmering light,
And their hearts started jumping
And thumping with fright.

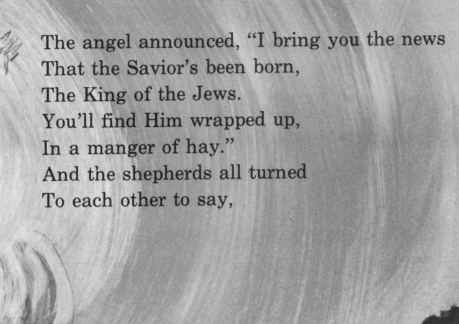

The angel announced, "I bring you the news
That the Savior's been born,
The King of the Jews.
You'll find Him wrapped up,
In a manger of hay."
And the shepherds all turned
To each other to say,

"Come on, let's go just as fast as we can."
And they dropped all their work
In the field and ran.

Oh, how delighted they were when they saw
The Baby, their King, asleep in the straw.
Their hearts were merry.
They bubbled with mirth.
And the news started spreading
All over the earth—

While the man at the inn
Kept working so hard
He missed what happened
In his own backyard.
But . . .

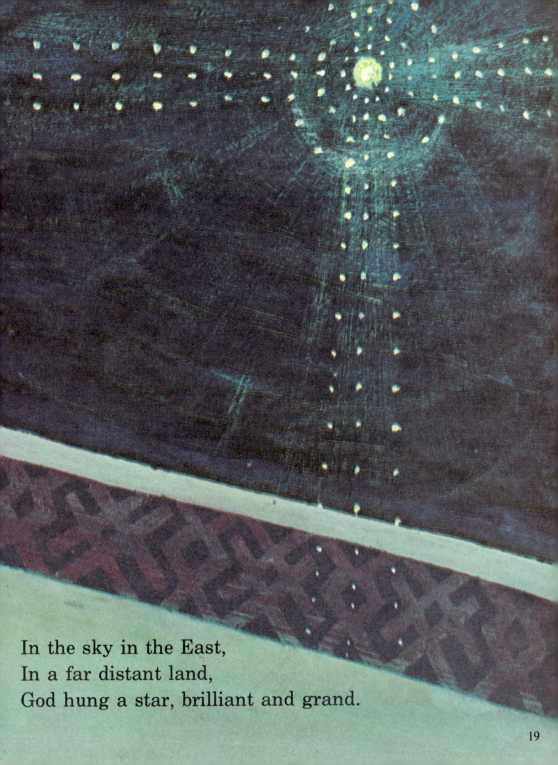

In the sky in the East,
In a far distant land,
God hung a star, brilliant and grand.

Three Wise Men said,
"It's to tell us the news
That a Savior's been born,
The King of the Jews."

They stopped and dropped
All the work they were doing,
For something of far more
Importance was brewing.

They loaded camels with treasures and gold
And all the supplies
That their saddles could hold.
Through hot, sandy deserts
They traveled each day.
The star was a compass to show the way.
Their friends and families
Were all left behind.

For months they continued,
One purpose in mind.

To them the very most wonderful thing
Was to worship the Baby,
Their Savior and King.

And then came a day they rounded the bend
That brought them with joy
To their journey's end.
As they bowed to the Child sent from above,
They gave Him their treasures.
They gave Him their love.

And Wise Men and shepherds
Had peace untold.
They had found God's Gift
More precious than gold.
All of them acted exactly the same.
They pushed aside
Everything else and came.

And the innkeeper? Well . . .
He's a different story.
He missed the peace, the joy and the glory.
He could have said, "Come. Eat at my table.
You take my room. *I'll* take the stable."
But it seems he was hurried
And worried and miffed
And never took time to find God's Gift.

That Gift is Jesus, a Savior, a Friend,
With life forever, that never will end.
He wants to enter your life and your heart
And stay there forever and never depart.
He knocks on your "door";
He's knocking today.
Will you tell Him, "Come in,"
Or turn Him away?

DEAR PARENTS:

Christmas has come to mean many things for each of us. But for most of us Christmas means rushing.

It's the season for rushing around in department and discount stores. It's the time for rushing out to get a tree and a wreath. We rush to get presents wrapped and cookies baked and children dressed for the Christmas program.

At Christmas most of us are the people who don't have time.

The innkeeper in the story was so busy he didn't have time for Jesus either. But the shepherds and Wise Men, when they heard about Jesus' birth, dropped everything and rushed to greet Him. To all people who take time for Him, Jesus gives eternity.

Or, looking at it another way, consider a matter of priorities. If someone knocked on the door with a beautiful gift—a box that contained a most treasured possession—one would certainly not brush him off, close the door, and go busily on with routine activities. Yet that is what many do to God, who holds out a priceless Treasure: peace, joy, forgiveness of sins—all wrapped up in Jesus.

Set aside time this Christmas season to read and discuss this Arch Book with your children. Don't hurry through it. Point out to them the importance of taking time to be with their Lord Jesus, who chose to be with them forever. That's what this story is all about.

THE EDITOR